ADOLESCENCE: THE SEARCH FOR THE SELF and WEAVING THE SOCIAL FABRIC OF THE CLASS

Two Lectures on Waldorf Education
by

Eugene Schwartz

RSCP

Cover Design: Theodore Mahle

Second printing 2001

ISBN 0-945803-11-7

The content of this book represents the view of the author and should in no way be taken as the official opinion or policy of Rudolf Steiner College or Rudolf Steiner College Press.

Book orders may be made through Rudolf Steiner College Bookstore. Tel. 916-961-8729, FAX 916-961-3032.

Rudolf Steiner College Press
9200 Fair Oaks Boulevard
Fair Oaks, CA 95628, U.S.A.

CONTENTS

A NOTE ON THE FOUR-FOLD HUMAN BEING

The lectures that follow were given to audiences who were familiar with the conceptual framework that underlies Waldorf education. The Waldorf philosophy and methodology is itself part of a more comprehensive world-picture known as Anthroposophy, introduced in this century by Rudolf Steiner (1861-1925).

A central idea underlying the Waldorf approach to education is that of the "four-fold human being." Rudolf Steiner presented this concept in a number of basic books (see the list at the end of this introduction) and elaborated upon it in thousands of lectures. What follows is a simplified outline of Steiner's complex picture.

That part of the human being which is perceived by the senses is what Steiner calls the Physical Body. At death, or through the severance of any part of that body from the whole (the cutting of the hair, the loss of a limb) the physical body will revert to the same chemical components as are to be found in the "lifeless," mineral world; hence the physical body can also be called the mineral body.

One stage higher than the physical body is the Etheric Body. Although invisible to our ordinary senses, the effects of this body are evident in all that sustains our life processes: Steiner also terms this member of our being the "life body." The etheric body bears within itself the "memory" of our form ("body of formative forces" is a third term used in describing it) and, in its interplay with our physical nature, carries our predisposition to health or illness. The immunological system recognized by modern medicine is one of the "effects" of the etheric body that manifest in the physical world.

The Astral Body is even more subtle in nature than the etheric body. It is this member which is often termed the "soul" or "soul body"; Steiner also identifies it as the body of wishes and desires. The etheric body gives us life, but it is the astral body which gives us sentience (however dreamlike it may be) and the capacity to move towards those objects or images we desire. Whether what we desire is as simple as food and shelter or as grandiose as world domination, the astral body is active.

That which allows the human being to experience his individual nature is termed by Steiner the "I" or Ego. This ego is at once the most individualized and the most universal aspect of our being. Hence everyone can call himself "I" but we can call no one else by that name. This ego "wears" the three other bodies like so many veils, expressing itself through them all yet remaining ineffably unique. It is this "I" which constitutes our spiritual nature, eternal and divine in essence.

In Steiner's anthroposophical world-view, the whole world is a macrocosmic reflection of the human microcosm. From this perspective, each of man's four bodies finds its echo in an "element" of nature. Thus, the physical body is of the nature of earth, the etheric body of the nature of water, the astral body of the nature of air and the ego is akin to fire. In terms of the "kingdoms of nature," we share our physical body with the mineral kingdom, our etheric body with the plant world, and our astral body with the animals. The ego is shared with no other kingdom: only the human being carries this "divine spark" into earthly life.

The ego ceaselessly works upon the three other bodies to spiritualize and perfect them. Its work will eventually result in the creation of new members of the human being. The ego's work upon the astral body will lead to the creation of the Spirit Self; its work upon the etheric body will result in the Life Spirit, and its spiritualization of the physical body will bring about the Spirit Man. Hence the ego stands as the "teacher" of the bodies of man, raising the lower into the higher by virtue of its eternal nature. In this respect the activity of the ego is the prototype of all human education.

In his numerous lectures to teachers, Rudolf Steiner elaborated upon the picture of the four-fold human being by emphasizing its chronological development.

Although we are four-fold beings from the moment we are born, each of our bodies fully expresses itself, i.e., "incarnates" at a different point in our life. From birth until age seven (or about the time of the second dentition) our physical body is most active, and the child's consciousness is bound up with processes of assimilation and growth, as the etheric body works upon the physical body from without. From seven to fourteen, the etheric body increasingly assumes the same contours as the physical body; it now dampens down its organic activity and its forces are metamorphosed into the newly-arising forces of memory. From fourteen to twenty-one, the astral body becomes dominant. The life of desire grows strong, as does the life of ideals; the ability to reason is born amidst the turmoil of the life of emotions. At twenty-one the ego is truly "born" within us. From this point on, education becomes increasingly a matter of self-education. The life-long process of becoming "adult" and fully human now begins.

Lest these simplified descriptions seem too rigid, it should be stressed that in the fullness of his work Rudolf Steiner repeatedly approached his four-fold picture from a multitude of perspectives and always stressed the mobility and transformative quality of the higher bodies of man. Only modes of thought which are in themselves mobile and fresh can comprehend the continually metamorphosing nature of the four-fold human being, but the careful and open-minded perusal of some of the books listed below may be a helpful first step.

Suggested books by Rudolf Steiner for further reading:

Theosophy (Anthroposophic Press, Hudson, NY)

An Outline of Occult Science (Anthroposophic Press)

At the Gates of Spiritual Science (Rudolf Steiner Press, London)

Study of Man (Rudolf Steiner Press)

ADOLESCENCE: THE SEARCH FOR THE SELF

A Lecture Given at the Austin Waldorf School, Austin, Texas, September 22, 1989

Dedicated to William Toole, the first Waldorf school teacher in Texas to take a class from grades one through eight.

Tonight marks the autumnal equinox, one of the two points in the course of the year when day and night are equal. The equinoxes, like the solstices, are determined by the relationship of the sun to the earth, that is, they are cosmic in nature. Thus when we say that autumn represents a point of balance, we are talking about a cosmic balance, and not necessarily an earthly state. Indeed, the immensely powerful hurricane which is raging over the east coast (Hurricane Hugo) is a typical autumnal phenomenon. There is so often unrest and imbalance just as earth and sun move into a state of equilibrium. It is as though the elements of air and water wish to rebel against the sun's cosmic rulership. Please keep those elements of air and water in mind; I'm going to give you a multiple choice test at the lecture's conclusion.

Of course, meteorologists will acknowledge that the powerful air flows and frontal movements that constitute an autumnal storm actually represent the release of pressure that builds up in a one-sided way over the course of the summer. As hurricanes circulate air and forcibly convey immense volumes of water from one part of the earth to another, they serve the work of long-range balance that underlies nature's household. Although the tumultuousness of the atmosphere appears from day-to-day to contradict the cosmic quality of the equinox, from a longer perspective we can see even the exception serving to support the rule.

Although the relationship of turmoil and balance may be a new idea to some of you, for those who are parents of adolescents it is a daily experience! One of the questions that we'll address tonight will be: is the turbulence of the adolescent years as necessary in human development as powerful storms are necessary in earthly weather? Now, Austin is in the "Sun Belt," and perhaps some of you have moved here because you are not enamored of powerful storms. Yet even you have your "northers" which bring chill, but refreshing winds, and rains that sweep in drenchingly from the Gulf with their attendant floods. Without those, everything in sight would be dried-up and dead. Do we find a correlation in human life?

Let's remain in Texas to find an answer to that question, and do it in a moseying, Texas sort of way. We'll try to picture two flowering plants that grow in this state. One is the State Flower, the Texas Bluebonnet. There are charming stories, both Native American and pioneer, concerning the origins of this flower, and well there might be, because it is a charming plant. The blue and white flowers, which appear in such profusion everywhere in the spring, seem to personify freshness, sweetness and purity. They look up to the sun, and their color seems to draw together the sun's light and the sky's soothing blueness. Couldn't we say that such flowers embody the essence of childhood, with its purity and goodness, and above all its openess to the world?

You'll have to forgive me for making such a trite comparison! Those of you who have had your children in a Waldorf school for several years have probably had teachers endlessly comparing childhood to the sprouting and flowering process. I remember a teacher beginning a parent evening in my school with such a comparison. A long-time school parent, connected with our school for almost two decades, turned to me and said, "It's that damn flower again!"

Our second flower is one which the Waldorf teachers don't use for purposes of comparison. It is the Jimson weed, or datura stramonium. The "thorn-apple," common in this state, is an especially tall member of the datura family, which befits a Texas plant. Unlike the bluebonnet, Jimson weed grows in partial shade; its flowers turn away from the light, and actually begin to turn in upon themselves, i.e. they invaginate before fruiting and seeding. And, unlike the bluebonnet, the Jimson weed is a poisonous plant.

I'm sure no teacher ever compared your child to a poisonous flowering plant before! You probably are thinking, "It takes a New Yorker to make a comparison like that!" Perhaps a sketch can help us understand this comparison:

The normal flowering plant is a physical-etheric entity, touched from outside by the astral world. This "touch" of astrality is expressed in the coloration of the flower and in the invagination of the fruiting process. The abnormal flowering plant, which is almost invariably poisonous, "sucks" astrality into itself at an earlier stage. It tries to imitate the animal, which bears its own astral body, which helps explain the animal-like patterns and forms that are sometimes found in poisonous flowers.

So those teachers were right, after all: a young child is like a normal flowering plant, for the child between birth and nine bears strong etheric forces, which lead to growth, love of light, and openness to the world. And what of the abnormal, poisonous plant? Here we see a picture of adolescence!

The "signature" of the astral body is the process of turning away from the light, closing off, invaginating and creating an individual space; hence the poisonous plant so often possesses flowers that close off and encapsulate the light or reject it altogether. Isn't this closing-off, rejecting, withdrawing gesture a perfect picture of certain stages of the teenage years? It is no wonder that Rudolf Steiner, the founder of the Waldorf school movement, once said that adolescence was a protracted illness.

Before we leave the plant world, I'd like to say something about the nature of the poisons that these over-astralized plants produce. Here we have a diagram of the molecular structure of a pyrrol, part of a porphyrin ring:

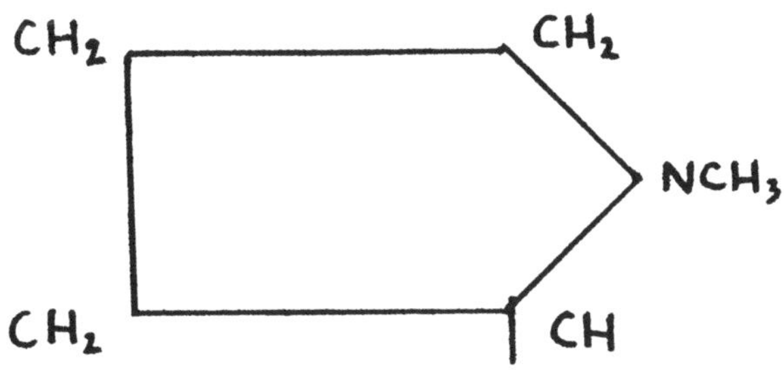

The porphyrin ring is the chemical basis of all alkaloids, or plant poisons. This particular ring comes from nicotine. We can see that its components include hydrogen, carbon and nitrogen. Hydrogen and carbon are found throughout the structure of normal plants, e.g. in carbohydrates—sugars and starches. Nitrogen, however, really belongs in the lower pole of the plant, in the roots where the plant meets the earth. But when the plant oversteps its bounds and pulls the astral world into itself, nitrogen appears throughout the plant, no longer in its rightful place, and helps to create a toxin. We can say that, in the plant, a physical body and an etheric, or life body, serve growth. The astral body, which is of the nature of soul, brings growth to an end and can even bear the forces of death in the form of poisons.

Here I have arranged four pyrrols to create a cross-like form:

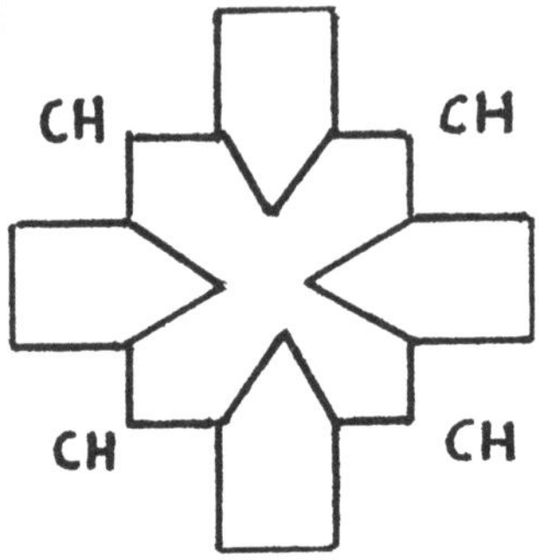

Another poison? In a way, yes, although you'll be surprised to learn that this poison is found in your own blood! It is remarkable to realize that our organism is full of substances which, were we to ingest them from without, would be deadly. All that prevents this potentially toxic substance from doing us in is the fact that, in our blood, iron stands in the center:

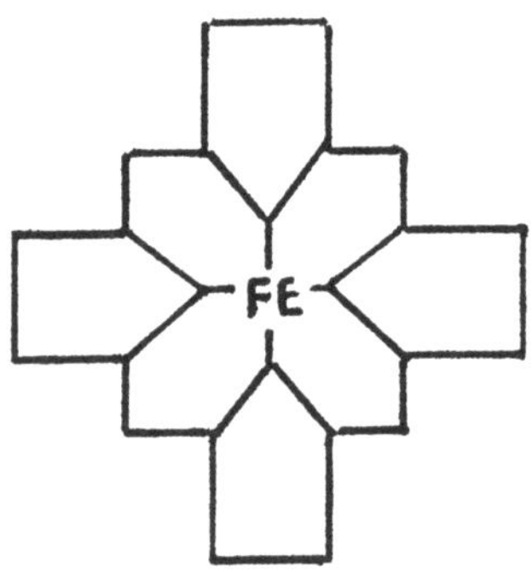

Now we have the structure of the heme, which is

the basis of hemoglobin, the foundation of our red blood. A "homeopathic dose" of iron counterbalances the toxicity of the alkaloid-like substances that surround it.

We are approaching Michaelmas, and I'm sure that many of your children are coming home with drawings or paintings of the Archangel Michael overcoming the Dragon, or perhaps they are vividly relating stories of that battle to you. Those of you who sent your children to a Waldorf school because you felt it was one of the only places on earth which cultivated serenity, social-mindedness and harmony among its students may now wonder, "What does this militaristic attack against an unarmed reptile—already an endangered species—have to do with world peace and environmental balance?"

The answer to that lies in our own blood. Insofar as we are red-blooded Americans, Texans, or just plain humans, we are forever battling to overcome the toxins within us. Our life is one of ceaseless conflict and overcoming. This is a conflict that goes on within the unconscious depths of our organism, within the very marrow of our bones. When the greatest spiritual leaders of the West wished to awaken mankind to this conflict, they presented it in pictorial form. The toxic substances (which we depict as a circular pyrrol ring) were seen as undifferentiated animal forces, bound to the earth and encircling their victim in a dragon-like hold. In their midst, ascending from a realm of light, was a figure in iron armor, holding an iron sword, vanquishing and taming the unruly forces of soul. As we look more closely at the adolescent, we shall see the particular importance of the changing nature of the blood and the heart at this age.

I bring all of this by way of introduction because this evening's topic is that stage of human development in which conflict and turmoil hold sway. Was it always so? I would contend that the tumultuous, "at-risk" scenario of adolescence that we take for granted nowadays is a phenomenon only about one hundred years old.

Amongst all great ancient cultures, the rites-of-passage marking a boy's or girl's entry into puberty and adolescence also marked his or her readiness to take on adult responsibilities, an expectation echoed even today in the words spoken by the thirteen year-old at the Jewish Bar Mitzvah: "Today I am a Man."

If we accept great dramas and novels as accurate sources of social mores, we see that, from the Middle Ages to the late nineteenth century, by fifteen or so an individual was ready to take on his or her pre-determined life tasks: apprenticeship, squire-hood, marriage and childbearing, etc. Even in Dickens' works, so sensitive to the changes in lifestyles wrought by the Industrial Revolution, we continue to find teenagers who are scaled-down adults with no "culture" of their own.

A work which I believe was seminal in alerting the world to the transformation of adolescence is a drama that is little-read or performed nowadays: Frank Wedekind's *Spring's Awakening*. Although the title is deceptively lovely, the drama is filled with the nineteenth century equivalent of "Sex, Drugs, and

Rock 'n' Roll": a litany of unfulfilled longings, powerful drives, cruelty and perversion. (It's the sort of thing your twelve year-olds might see in a PG-rated movie!) The play follows a group of young adolescents through their experiences in the restrictive Prussian schoolroom and their wild existence outside of school. What was unique about Wedekind's approach was that the drama is written from the youngsters' point of view—it was his genius to recognize that there is such a thing as an "adolescent point of view."

Although Wedekind wrote the play in 1890, so shocking were the reviews of those who had read the text that it took sixteen years before a modified version was produced in Berlin. A 1917 New York performance was almost stopped by the City Commissioner, and it was not until 1965, after two years of negotiations with the Lord Chamberlain, that the play had its first public performance in London!

An English reviewer of the 1917 performance wrote,

> *Thank Heaven that we in England have always grown up too slowly and set too much store by childish pursuits and games!*

Among those present at the 1906 performance in Berlin was the former drama critic Rudolf Steiner, who recognized immediately the coruscating truth that shone through the darkness of Wedekind's picture of the world's awakening to adolescence.

To approach the great soul transformations that

are experienced by the adolescent, we will go by way of the more evident physical changes that occur at this life period, and then focus on the less visible, inner metamorphoses that play their own profound role.

This may seem to be a strange approach for a Waldorf teacher to take, since in the minds of many, Waldorf education is synonymous with "soul education," an approach that takes us away from the body to the "higher things in life."

Actually, among those "higher things" the physical body stands first and foremost. In the first seven years of life, Waldorf educators leave the child's soul and spirit free to work on molding that very physical body, and in the second seven years we try to help that physical body become ever more an image of the soul by cultivating its rhythmic processes. Now, as we approach the third seven-year period, we must again look to the physical body for those signposts which can help to guide us in our understanding. For those of you interested in a more detailed psychological study of adolescence, I can heartily recommend *Between Form and Freedom* by Betty Staley (Hawthorne Press 1988).

The newborn child is "all head"; not, of course, in the intellectual sense, but in physical terms. The limbs are tiny in proportion to the head of the infant, and, like the young child's drawing of a person, seem to branch out from that important sphere. We know that early adolescence has commenced when the hands and feet start to grow rapidly. Now it is the head's turn to appear small in relationship to the large extremities, whose growth is next transferred to the arms and legs and thence to the trunk. After seven years or so of well-proportioned, rhythmic growth, the youngster must now contend with limbs that are big and not always responsive to his will.

The head is that pole of our body which enters least into a relationship with earthly weight and gravity; Rudolf Steiner once characterized the head as a nobleman who rides in a carriage. Hence the young child, who is so cosmic in nature, would have the head-pole dominant. The adolescent is fully "touching down onto the earth," becoming aware of and oriented to gravity and density; hence it will be his extremities and limbs, which are most "in touch" with the earth, which will lead the way down.

The clumsiness and gawkiness that characterizes adolescence has its charm, but it can be exasperating to have those heirloom dishes dropping to the floor every evening at cleanup, or to watch as chairs tip over and candelabras topple every time your youngster gets up from the table! I have heard that those astronauts who walked upon the moon had similar experiences upon their return to the earth. Having lived in a world where greater levity reigned, they had to find their way down and back to the greater confinement of our weighty planet.

I've taken many opportunities to observe teenagers from a variety of educational backgrounds, to see how they relate to this "earthly landing." After years of careful, scientific observations at major shopping malls on Saturday mornings, skating rinks on Saturday afternoons and movie theatres on

Saturday nights—you can tell that I'm the parent of teenagers!—I've come to the following conclusion: my experience has been that, on the whole, youngsters who have gone through some years of the Waldorf Lower School are less clumsy and better able to carry their new length and weight than their peers from other school settings. I am sure that an important reason for this less painful integration of body and soul is the eurythmy that they have had over the years.

If the growth of the first seven years is above all growth of the inner organs, while the growth of the second seven years has more to do with the harmonization of the organs' functions through the rhythmic organization, we can say that the growth of the third seven year period is very much linked to the elongation and hardening of the long bones. This is why Waldorf schools wait until eighth grade to teach directly about the human skeleton, although we pave the way from without through sixth grade Mineralogy and seventh grade Mechanics.

Only at age fourteen do we find that the child's relationship to his own skeleton can become conscious and somewhat objective, as newly-lengthened limbs become "foreign objects" and "growing pains" awaken the youngster to processes that were once imperceptible. As these downward-drawing forces gain dominance, the youngster's center of gravity shifts, moving from the cervical vertebrae to the sacrum.

It all adds up to a hard and rapid falling into earthly life, from which no one can escape without a few bruises! We should not expect that it is going to be different with our children, unless we want them to remain little children all their lives. The struggles of adolescence are a path to experiencing our full humanness. What was once provided by the tribal ordeal or by priestly fiat is now provided by life itself: in our age, adolescence has become its own rite of passage.

A key to understanding the nature and significance of this "fall of man" in adolescence is Rudolf Steiner's revelation that time moves in two directions. I have discussed this more fully in lectures that you have heard on the "Nine Year-Old Change" (see Rhythms and Turning Points in the Life of the Child, Rudolf Steiner College Publications, 1989). As we learned there, a stream of time moves from the past towards the future, bearing our physical and etheric being and all that connects us with heredity.

Another stream of time moves from the future towards the past, bearing tidings from the astral world and the Ego, awakening us to all that is of the nature of our individuality.

There is little value in looking to the past for explanations of an adolescent's behavior; it has far more to do with the future. I hope that this helps to alleviate some of your collective guilt!

I am sure that we have all known children who were brought up "correctly," whether judged by "Waldorf" standards (whatever those are) or other standards, and who turned out to be utterly confused and fuming teenagers. Now and then we find youngsters whose early childhood was "all wrong": though products of broken homes, spoiled, or neglected, they become level-headed and self-reliant in their adolescent years. I'm not suggesting that you go home and begin neglecting your children, but I am saying that the nature of the individuality is a mystery, and that adolescence cannot be understood at all without a recognition of the power of the Self, which streams into the present from the future.

And what of the "model child," who has been brought up with care and solicitude, who passes through the crisis of the nine-year-old change with unruffled feathers and glides with apparent aplomb through the stormy seas of the teenage years? Here we have a real cause for concern! Steiner tells us that every child is a "model child" before age seven, for his physical body at that time is a model of his parents' bodies, "lent" to the child to help him gain a foothold in the physical world. The second seven years represent an effort on the part of the child to cast off the model body, through such means as losing the beautiful first set of teeth, through the childhood illnesses and through the minor rebellions that occur with especial power at ages nine to ten.

The child who is unable to perform this casting off remains a "model child" through the second seven-year period, which means that he or she remains entwined in the forces of heredity. Such a child continues to live strongly according to the forces of imitation (which are most appropriate up to age seven) and authority (appropriate up to age fourteen) well through the teenage years, without directly confronting the critical question, "Do I really want to incarnate in my own body?"

We can say that real growth and development in human life represents, to use the expression of the economist Christopher Budd, an emancipation through denial. The youngster who, upon attaining the teenage years, suddenly questions her family's habits and values, who demands "her own space"—both in the physical and emotional sense—is undergoing this process of emancipation. As is the case with all new steps in human development, including childbirth, this is a process at once exhilarating and painful.

The problem of the persistence of the model body has been exacerbated by the diminishing incidences of childhood illnesses such as measles and chicken pox. Such illnesses allowed the child to literally "cast off" his old skin and to pass through the febrile "trial of fire," emerging phoenix-like, as a new being. We must work in a more conscious way to allow the child to pull away from the forces of mere heredity and strive towards the creation of his own body in the image of the spirit.

By adolescence, the second stream begins to assert ever greater power in our life. Can we find a correlation to this in the collective life of humanity? We find it in the story of the Fall of Man! You will recall that Waldorf students hear this story in third grade, when they are rehearsing, as it were, the roles that they will play as adolescents. The Fall is one of those seminal events in earthly evolution that at once should not have happened and had to happen.

Rudolf Steiner tells us that it was at this time that certain spiritual beings endowed man with the astral body, long before he was ready to control its powerful nature. To this day, the astral body, and our accompanying sense of self, are "given over" to us before we are ready to receive them. Indeed, Steiner says that if those progressive beings who rightfully rule evolution had their way, we would not come into our selves in this way until we were twenty-one years old. According to the picture he gives in The Mission of the Folk-Souls, the progressive spiritual beings intended that human beings would spend the first and last third of their lives in the spiritual world, and only fully incarnate on the earth from ages twenty to forty.

Now you may argue that you know many people who are twenty-one and older who act like adolescents, but I don't believe that this is what Steiner meant! Had matters gone according to plan (which they rarely do, even when the plans are made by the Hierarchies) human beings would be sleepy and dreamy beings for the first twenty-one years of life, with no possibility of doing evil, which also means, with no possibility of freedom. The earlier, premature incorporation of the astral body gives us the potential to be free—a possibility which is not lost on the adolescent who first experiences it.

This new-found potential to "be as gods" was inexorably followed by the consequences of suffering, illness and death. This, too, we find repeated in human life as the child crosses the threshold of adolescence. Ages fourteen to eighteen are so often marked by a new fragility which somehow coexists with growing physical massiveness and strength; by an uncompromising attitude towards people and the world which inevitably leads to suffering, and, above all, by a sudden interest in, we might even say a fascination with death.

Here is a composition by an eighth grader. The assignment was to give a third-person description of a summer experience:

> *She heard pouring rain, gushing from the clouds, beat upon her windows. Her teeth chattered, but it wasn't from the cold, for the rest of her body shook too. A cold cloth, dampened with water, had been wrapped about her head. She was lying on her bed, staring up, praying to the water that was running in rivulets down the glass pane, to the water that dripped across her face, to the water that soaked through the floral-spattered paper cup clenched in her right hand. She trembled again. In her left hand, her palm swallowed up a spherical purple crystal. She prayed to that also.*
>
> *"Please let me be O.K. Let me get better. Water, you are the element that has proven to be faithful to me. So help me now, please. Oh God, Oh Spirit of Water, please, to the crystal I am clutching, let me stop feeling this way!"*
>
> *She shook. The crystal and the cup of water surged vibrations into her hands and up her arms, adding to the shaking that she was experiencing. The evening dimmed and the sky*

was a slate of grey. The winds howled; it was a dirge. She hoped it belonged to someone else. The trees were black figures, silhouettes, swaying a dangerous distance from the earth. The soil! It was a traitor, for it had not yet offered its comfort to the terrified girl trembling viciously on the bed.

The power went out. It was dark in the messy room, the floor strewn with clothes, once tried on and discarded. Candles were brought in, dripping wax cascades, making a pretty waterfall, frozen in a moment of time.

Fire was her friend. Her sign was a flame-bitten one, so she felt at home. Comforted, loved by the Moon, the Water, the Fire; she was like night anyway, working at the shadowed hours, tiring with the day. Always it had been so.

She began to feel relaxed. The sickening convulsion ceased. Gazing at the candle's flame, her features ringed with sweat, she felt the night was over her, flooding her eyelids and her soul. She fell asleep.

Just as the stream that bears our physical/etheric nature comes from out of the spiritual world and unites us with our pre-birth experiences, so this astral/ego stream comes from out of the spiritual world in the opposite direction and awakens us to our future life after death. Every adolescent has a delicate, evanescent premonition of his future death. If we view death as a horrible cessation of the comfortable earthly life to which we've grown accustomed, then of course we'll try to distract our teenager in every way possible from having such thoughts! If we recognize that death is, in its truest nature, an opening into the spiritual world, an insight into our eternal individuality, then we will understand why something akin to a longing for death arises in the healthiest adolescent soul.

Yet there is another side to the allure that death holds for the adolescent. I would call this the shadow side of adolescence: the wish not to have been born. When the physical and etheric bodies of the growing child have not been sufficiently strengthened through the first fourteen years of life, when a love for the world, for life, indeed, what can only rightfully be termed a love of God has not been awakened in the child's soul, it is very difficult for him to bear the power of the astral body. The longing for death that arises in such a case is not the healthy wish to fully become one's self, but rather the fearful urge to escape one's destiny and seek oblivion.

The alarming rise in the teenage suicide rate and the emergence of illnesses and social problems that can lead to death, e.g., anorexia and drug addiction, point too clearly to the fact that we are not dealing with this "death-wish" in the right way. The point is not to avoid it, but rather to prepare the growing child so that he will be strong enough to say "Yes!" to an ever-fuller and deeper incarnation into his body and into earthly life.

The Waldorf school curriculum represents just such a path towards healthy incarnation. Rudolf Steiner has said that, by cultivating gratitude and love in the first fourteen years, we prepare the youngster to face the duty of living on and making something of the rest of his life. This is a duty that should be a joy to undertake! By awakening the child to the wonder and multiplicity of all that mankind has achieved through stories, sagas, myths and the study of history, we recall to his soul the high calling that is inherent in our human nature.

A young person who does not get to study history is like a ship without tiller or anchor, cast about by the meaningless storms of modern life. An adolescent who does learn history, but learns it only as a progression of wars and treaties, dynasties and parliaments, is hardly better off. What teenagers need are examples of living, breathing individuals who faced the threshold of death—which is really the threshold of life—and said "yes" to their duty and destiny. Only then can the power of the astral body be harnessed in the billowing sails of a well-captained ship!

This is why Waldorf schools stress biography as the basis of the study of history in the middle school years. For example, between the late seventh and early eighth grades, Waldorf students learn the complex story of the Reformation almost exclusively through the biography of Martin Luther. As he leaves the comforting domain of the "Mother Church" and chooses to follow the challenge of his own thorny destiny, Luther discovers the meaning of his own individuality. This is what one student made of this experience:

Lying on the hard wooden bed with only a threadbare woolen blanket to keep his gaunt body warm, he realized that for the first time in his life he felt annoyance at his discomfort. "These are not good thoughts," he told himself. Yet he did not want to do penance. He did not want to climb stairs on his bare knees or wear a shirt lined with the coarse hair of boars. Was it not punishment enough to be tried in front of a court for heresy? He, one of the most pious of priests! Then pictures of things he had done in his life flashed before him: pictures of his hard-working parents barely able to survive, trying to make enough money to send him to the many schools he had attended. Perhaps he should have been a lawyer as his father had wished. He thought of that unworthy man Tetzel, the one selling Indulgences and telling lies, forgiving people for sins they had not yet committed. The anger in him was rising more and more for every second that he thought of Tetzel.

He needed to get himself together. Tomorrow, for him, would be the day of judgment. Tomorrow he would be released as innocent or convicted and perhaps burned as guilty. Pondering these thoughts, he began to form a speech in his mind, then threw it away as he would a bone after all the meat had been eaten.

Suddenly a realization dawned on him: he could either do what he felt to be right and be considered a heretic, be excommunicated and possibly burned at the stake—or he could go against his heart, take back all the words he had written or said and be a free man. He was torn, his mind logically telling him what to do, and his heart insisting that he tell the truth. The sun would rise soon and he knew that he would have to make a decision before daylight.

As the sun rose, so there rose a resolution in Martin Luther. Soon after it grew light, two guards entered Martin Luther's room, helped him from his bed and quietly brought him to the courtroom. As he entered, the room fell silent. Martin Luther was brought up to the wooden platform where the prosecutor repeated his question of the day before: "Do you admit that these books you have written preach heresy?"

In a steady voice, with resolution firm in his heart, Martin Luther replied that not he, but the Pope was a heretic, for claiming to be better than Jesus Christ and to be able to talk to the saints and to God—

"NO!" cried the Emperor Charles, who presided over the trial.

"Wait, let me finish!" said Martin Luther, whose closing sentence was, "Here I stand, I can do no other!"

The room was silent, for people were so shocked at what he had said. Martin Luther got up and walked out of the courtroom. Back in his room, although Martin Luther was frightened, he knew things would work out.

As this composition demonstrates, the deeds

and sufferings of an heroic individual can serve as an objective correlative for the soul experiences of a modern adolescent. If teenagers cannot find heroes, they will creates heroes, as the almost mythical qualities they bestow on rock musicians, sports figures and movie stars can attest. How much better to learn about real heroes, who can fire a youngster's soul with a yearning for something more than getting high or owning a Ferrari!

Perhaps you noticed how often the heart is mentioned in this composition:

> *. . . he could either do what he felt to be right and be considered a heretic, be excommunicated and possibly burned at the stake—or he could go against his heart, take back all the words he had written or said and be a free man . . .*
>
> *He was torn, his mind logically telling him what to do, and his heart insisting that he tell the truth . . .*
>
> *In a steady voice, with resolution firm in his heart, Martin Luther replied that not he, but the Pope was a heretic . . .*

Within the body and soul of the thirteen year-old who wrote this composition was arising a re-formation no less turbulent than the Reformation begun by Martin Luther. In a remarkable lecture on The Human Heart (Dornach, May 26, 1922) Rudolf Steiner spoke of the significant transformation that occurs in the heart at the time of puberty. The old "model" etheric heart decays, and in its place arises a new heart, which has the role of uniting our cosmic intentions with our human deeds. The heart now becomes the junction of the streams emanating from the etheric world and from the astral world, the "crossing point" in time. As Steiner says, "This is the point where the cosmos—the cosmic process—is joined to the karma of man."

As the youngster intuitively senses, the most important decisions in life—whether Luther's, or her own—will from this moment be made in the heart, as the newly-born individuality tries to bring karmic necessity in line with earthly deeds. No other organ in the body undergoes such a dramatic re-formation as does the heart.

The heart is, of course, intimately related to the circulation of the blood, which is also undergoing important changes as adolescence approaches. It is the blood which bears most strongly the impress of the "I," the human ego, which is streaming in from the future. And, as I mentioned earlier, within the blood there is a ceaseless battle between toxins and antitoxins, between death and life, which I characterized imaginatively as the battle of the Dragon and Michael.

Here is a graph taken from *The Anthroposophical Approach to Medicine, Volume I,* by Friedrich Husemann and Otto Wolff:

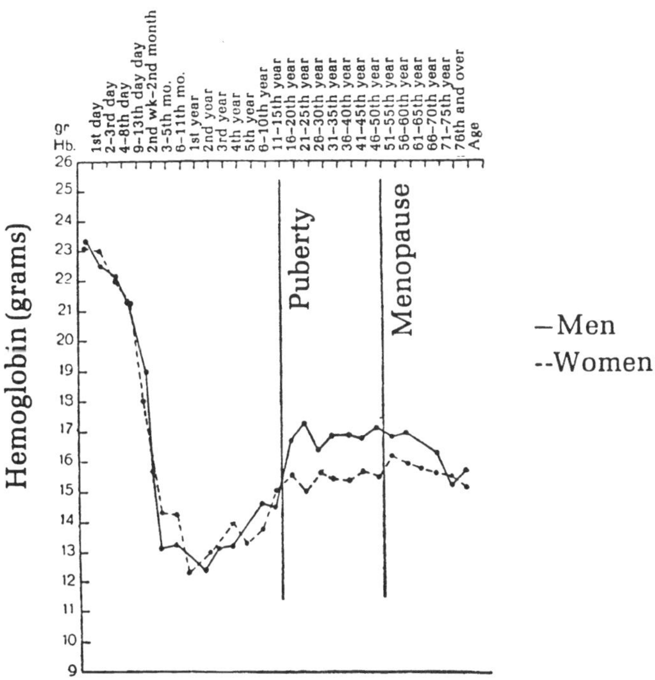

We can see how, particularly in the case of boys, the iron level of the blood, expressed as hemoglobin, rises dramatically. The poet Novalis once said, "Wherever children are, there is the Golden Age;" we might add, "Wherever teenagers are, there is the Age of Heavy Metal!" I don't mean this only in the musical sense, but also as evidenced by the increasing "weight" of iron found in the blood. Although it is "heavy," this iron brings with it light-bearing forces which balance the alkaloids in the blood.

When this balance cannot be maintained, when

the alkaloids proliferate in spite of iron's power, the organism "casts them out," just as in the biblical "War in Heaven" Michael cast out the rebellious angels. The alkaloids then shift their scene of activity from the inner domain of the blood and become more active in the outer domain of the skin. Acne and other teenage skin problems are one sign of this inner struggle between iron and alkaloids; body odor is another. The painful self-consciousness resulting from both of these teenage difficulties is, of course, difficult to bear. On the other hand, it is far better for the long-term health of the individual that the alkaloids be cast out onto the periphery than allowed to fester within.

The next chart, taken from Walter Holtzapfel's *Children's Illnesses*, looks at the blood from another perspective:

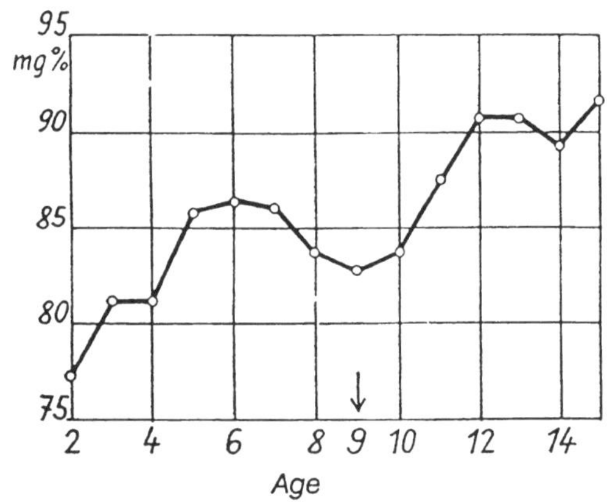

Blood sugar level in childhood. Average of 700 children, grouped according to age (I.B. Mayer).

Steiner has said that blood-sugar serves as the foundation for ego-consciousness, for knowing oneself to be an individual, an "I." We see how dramatically the blood-sugar level drops at age nine, the age I have characterized as a sort of "sneak preview" of adolescence. Then we see another drop at age fourteen, when adolescence comes in full force.

As any of us can attest from our own experience, a drop in blood sugar level makes us weak, uncertain and insecure. Ages nine to ten and thirteen to fifteen are periods when the youngster is especially "at risk" in this regard. We should not be surprised at the ceaseless craving for sweets that arises in adolescence, since an external source of sugar can to some extent compensate for the inner loss of this ego-bearing substance. This is also one of those situations in which ideas that are so taken for granted among progressively-minded parents, e.g., "sugar is always harmful," "less sugar is always better than more," etc. may have to be modified or discarded. At age three or eleven, sugar-filled treats may be unnecessary, but at age fourteen they may be of help to a youngster whose inner life needs sugar's sustaining power.

So we see how complex and contradictory a battlefield our blood becomes at adolescence: its hemoglobin content rises, expressing an ever-stronger urge to incarnate, while its sugar content drops, bringing an uncertainty of the spirit and an unclear sense of self. How many of you have lived through a scene such as this? You've watched your son playing soccer all Saturday morning. Though weighed down with padding and heavy cleats, he has run at breakneck speeds for hours, picking himself up again and again after collisions and falls, his spirits undiminished through it all. A day or two later, he comes home and negligently drops his coat on the kitchen floor.

"Please pick up your coat," you say (you're an especially polite parent!).
"Later," he says, dropping into a chair.
"Pick it up now," you insist.
"I'm busy," he says, tearing open a bag of corn chips.
"Now!"
"Come on, Mom, I'm too tired now!"

Yes, we all learn to live with such contradictions! But it is important to see how these outer "comedies of errors" are accurate pictures of the inner workings of soul and spirit right down to the molecular structure of the blood.

Let us return to the image of the plant and its relationship to the astral world, but this time examine it in terms of warmth. In general, before the astral world can touch the plant, the summer must have progressed far enough that days and nights are consistently warm. Warmth is the precondition for the emergence of most flowers, while the seeds that eventually arise can even "store" warmth in the form of fiery oils.

In the adolescent, the forces of warmth that are a precondition for the reception of the astral body manifest in the development of fats. The connection between the astral world, human warmth and fat used to be well understood; think, for instance, of those corpulent "smiling Bodhisattvas" or the generously proportioned goddesses who inhabit the light-filled canvases of Reubens or Titian.

Nowadays, one of the mottoes by which we live is, "You can never be too rich or too thin." Our particular standard of beauty in the West—which, like most standards of beauty, will eventually fade and be replaced by another standard—calls for adult women who are tall and thin. While I don't wish to quibble with an idea that keeps thousands of people gainfully employed in beauty salons and weight-control clinics, I do want to look at how things stand in this sphere for the adolescent, particularly the adolescent girl.

We find, for example, that before the onset of menses one fifth of a girl's weight is fat. At the time of the first period, this proportion increases to one fourth; by age fifteen, a healthy girl's weight will be about one third fat. These are so-called "normal" proportions. I would suspect that in an urban, upper-middle class group of adolescent girls in America many girls would be under pressure not to attain the state of one-third fat. Yet, just as outer sunlight and warmth are necessary for the blossoming and ripening process in the plant, so is inner warmth, i.e. fat, a healthy precondition for the monthly "ripening process" expressed in the menstrual cycle.

I'm glad that these words offer some relief to a number of you—I presume that you are smiling on behalf of your daughters, rather than yourselves. We must understand, of course, that not all fat is created equal! The condition of fat within the organism of a fourteen year-old is quite different from that of the fat within an adult body. Within the youngster's organism, we find that every day almost half of that fat content is transported to the liver, and there transformed into protein, sugar or other substances needed for the body's activities; at the same time, "new" fat is deposited to maintain the body's mantle of warmth.

We should think of the adolescent's body as being a candle or torch, ceaselessly consuming its own substance to create the warmth and light of human consciousness. It is the fiery nature of adolescence itself which keeps fat in a dynamic relationship to other bodily processes and thus maintains its healthy proportion in the human being. For the teenager fat is thus a picture of the individuality's striving to form, break down and re-form substance until the ego finds a reflection of its own image.

In the adult, however, the fire dies down, leaving at best glowing embers and memories of youth. Liver activity slows down—indeed, the liver itself shrinks dramatically in the course of a lifetime—and fat assumes an increasingly static relationship to the body. After our mid-thirties, fat is no longer a protective mantle for the spirit, but can become what Rudolf Steiner called a wall against the spiritual. This is not to say that trimming our excess fat will automatically make us more spiritual! Rather, insofar as we can keep alive the fiery idealism of our adolescent years, the openness to the new and the sense of life's golden promise and potential—insofar as we take seriously our spiritual strivings—to that extent will our body's fat remain relatively dynamic rather than inert.

I'm not proposing yet another weight-loss gimmick here, but I am merely stating the obvious: that which we call aging is profoundly connected to the hardening of fats within our body. Those fats are intimately related to our ideals, our aspirations and higher feelings, to all that is of the nature of warmth and enthusiasm within us. This is what the adolescent has to offer his parents and teachers—another chance to grow ardent and exhilarated about life itself! Teaching or bringing up adolescents may not make us "too thin" (and it certainly won't leave us "too rich") but if approached in the right way it can help us to stay young in spirit.

We can understand from this that, while efforts at "weight control" may be necessary for an adult, it is the cultivation of idealism and a positive attitude towards life that will help maintain the healthy mobility of fats within the body of the teenager. This in turn leads us to the problem of anorexia nervosa. I'm sure that every one of you knows someone, perhaps someone near and dear, who has suffered from this contemporary illness. I would like to share with you a description of the anorexic youngster given by Dr. Holtzapfel in his book, *Children's Illnesses:*

These children—mostly girls—defend themselves

with all their might against the descent into matter—against growing up in general. The disease begins with loss of appetite, avoidance of particular foods, especially fats, until gradually almost all nourishment is refused. A strong ascetic overtone becomes evident. The girls reject the bodily changes bound up with puberty and attempt, via radical fasts, to prevent the development of the female form or to force it to regress. They are astoundingly successful. The monthly period which has already begun, ceases. There is such an extreme wasting that the figure, little more than skin and bones, reminds one of what one might imagine the Egyptian mummies to look like. To remain a child, not wanting to accompany others on this journey to materiality, this is a desire not infrequently seen in children of this age (also very common is the opposite: such children want to grow up as fast as possible!), albeit not in the radical form seen in this disease. Here in the body itself the protest, denial and opposition of this age is readily visible. In opposition to the lassitude of their obese counterparts, these children are over-zealous, altruistic, with a strong social inclination . . .

We can say that the putting on of weight, the building up of an increased fat level in the body, is a way of saying, "Yes!" to the incarnation process. The healthy child accepts the burden of earthly substance, the material cross that we all must bear.

It is an observable fact that girls experience

puberty differently than boys. Whereas the girl's descent into matter is marked by visible changes on the periphery, e.g., the increase of fat, the development of the breasts from out of the skin, the boy's descent is rendered most obvious by the change in voice. While through adolescence a girl's voice may change by a tone or two, the boy descends a full octave. As his voice "deepens" and his limbs become more muscular, we can experience in the growing boy the truth of St. John's image of "the Word becoming flesh."

Another marked difference between boys and girls at this age is the intensity with which they approach the threshold of adolescence. For girls, puberty and early adolescence are times of great turmoil and inner distress. Most Waldorf teachers would agree that classes with a majority of girls in them are easier to teach and manage for the first five or six grades, but by seventh grade the daily emotional upheaval more than balances out the serenity of the first few years.

Yet the very intensity of her pubescent/adolescent years gives the girl an opportunity to "work through" her experience in a more complete way. The boy tends to work through puberty slowly and inwardly (this is relatively speaking, of course), but because of his lack of intensity, he does not work through adolescence as fully as the girl. Indeed, American life offers much evidence of the fact that most boys never outgrow adolescence!

The physiology, or "health and hygiene" classes that the youngsters have in seventh grade (followed by anatomy—with a stress on osteology—in eighth grade) deal primarily with nourishment. The students follow the course of foodstuffs from the moment they are perceived by the senses until the food loses its substantial identity and becomes part of the human body. In the course of such studies, we look at the teeth, the tongue, the alimentary canal, the stomach, liver, etc. but we do not discuss the sexual functions.

You may wonder, "In this age of sexually-transmitted diseases and teenage pregnancies, isn't it downright irresponsible to ignore sex education in the upper grades of the elementary school? Isn't it dangerous for adolescents to remain ignorant concerning these all-important changes going on in their physical and emotional lives?"

I'll try to speak to this justifiable concern from a Waldorf teacher's perspective, but I first want to share a personal observation. For more than a decade, I've received the Fisher Scientific Educational Catalog. Fisher is the largest of the school science equipment suppliers and is hence a good indicator of new trends in science education. Over these twelve years I've noticed how the catalog section on sex education has grown almost exponentially. First there were books and charts, then "audio-visual aids," then transparent plastic models of the human abdomen, then videotapes and software—the media became ever more "high-tech," although the content, I presume, remained about the same as it has always been!

One reason for the proliferation of materials on

the subject was that, while in late seventies sex education was a somewhat controversial subject limited to high schools, by the nineties it had become a required subject in public schools throughout the nation for virtually all grade levels.

It is interesting that another section of the catalog has also evinced such dramatic growth: this is the section on Sexually Transmitted Diseases. It, too, now offers the gamut of media from simple-to-read books to videotapes and computer programs. The growth of this section, however, has a lot to do with the fact that there are many more sexually-transmitted diseases today than there were in the late seventies! Whereas in those "innocent" days high school juniors and seniors learned a little bit about syphilis and gonorrhea, today's fifth graders are responsible for understanding the causes, prevention and treatment of not only those "classic" venereal diseases, but crabs, herpes and AIDS as well. The very young study primers on protecting themselves from sexual abuse. Along with this, pubescent youngsters are expected to understand how to choose the best method of contraception in any given situation. With a course load like that, how do they ever find the time to do their geography homework?

An interesting phenomenon, isn't it? An ever-increasing concern for sex education and an ever-growing incidence of sexually-transmitted diseases.. . And which came first? The conventional answer would be that it is the growth of sexually-related problems—all of them stemming from ignorance of human sexuality—which has led conscientious educators to wish to replace this ignorance with knowledge and understanding.

I would look at it in another way. We all know the power of the thoughts and images that we bear within our souls; many a New Age workshop capitalizes on the "power of creative visualization." We adults already have dampened down our imaginative life to a great extent. In the case of a child, the pictures he receives from outside are still imbued with such life and energy that they exert a formative force over the child's soul and body. To awaken a child to sexual processes—especially through the use of the biological/mechanical presentations so often used today—causes sexuality to assume a much larger role in the child's life than would otherwise be the case. Any process in our organism which oversteps its rightful boundaries leads to illness. If sexuality assumes this aggrandizing role in a child's life, then that child may well be far more open to sexually-related ailments in later years.

I realize that what I have said runs right against the grain of the most progressive and enlightened educational thinking of our time, and some of you may find this unsettling. You would be justified in next asking, "If you don't believe in sex education, what do you do to prepare and protect innocent children for our sexually-oriented and often exploitative world? And is there ever a time when sex is discussed in a Waldorf school?"

When the writer M.C. Richards was asked whether Waldorf schools prepare children for the modern world she answered, "Can any school prepare a child for the modern world?" Perhaps not, but I would say that if anything can help, the very best preparation for living in this or any other world is to help the child cultivate love in his being. One of the most disturbing aspects of contemporary sex education is that it treats sex as a subject in and of itself, separate from the feelings of affection, longing and love that should surround it and enfold it. The lower school years in the Waldorf school represent an ongoing effort to help each child develop love for the world and his or her fellow human being.

The assumption in our intellectual age is that knowledge of a danger automatically protects us from that danger, and that more knowledge will protect us more. And if there is already a lot of knowledge concerning the danger and it still hasn't gone away (as with drug abuse) then the problem must be that the knowledge has to circulate more widely. Rarely is it recognized that knowledge is essentially related to head activity; adolescents, in particular, are far more likely to act on the basis of their feelings.

Love is to the heart and feelings what knowledge is to the head and thinking. Youngsters who have had love awakened in their souls—love for their parents, love for their teachers and love for their classmates—not only will have knowledge of the dangers they must face, but the wisdom to act sensibly in the face of them. Insofar as Waldorf students are part of this world, we find experimentation with sex and substances among them, too. Our experience has been that in most cases the influence of their education provides them with the forces needed to prevent experimentation from becoming habituation.

In the seventh grade Waldorf students learn about the Renaissance, studying it especially through the lives and works of the great artists of that time. Here are reproductions of two paintings; one is a medieval depiction of the Virgin and Child, and the other is one of the masterpieces of the early Renaissance, Botticelli's *The Birth of Venus*. We could say that the healthy attitude of the pre-teen toward sex is not unlike that of the medieval painter. Sexuality, which our post-Freudian culture tells us is on everyone's mind and has always been on everyone's mind, was clearly not on the mind of the Mary painter. His concern is with facial expression and soul gesture, with a being who has not fully incarnated into a "fallen" body.

You'll notice, of course, the greater dynamism and freedom in the Botticelli painting, and you can see that its central figure is unclothed. The Renaissance represents for human history what early adolescence represents for the individual. Painters like Botticelli were awakening to the spirituality of the physical world itself, which included the human physical body. Venus was the Roman goddess of Love, yet notice how demurely she stands, born out of the elements of water, air and light in all of their purity. Love is here intimately related to the quality of chastity—not celibacy, mind you, but chastity, the "holding back" of sexual forces for the sake of something higher.

When was the last time that chastity was presented in a sex education course? Well, we don't "present" it either, or even talk much about it—it is here, in the art work itself, and such a picture is worth more than a thousand words. Through the cultivation of beauty, as well as love, Waldorf students are strengthened in regard to mastering their own awakening sexuality and all that to which the world will force them to awaken.

In the seventh grade drawings that surround us in this room we see ample evidence of the adolescent's ability to respond to the beauty of Renaissance art works and to reproduce them. Imagine how profoundly the soul of a thirteen year-old is engaged when he or she is striving to copy the lines of a Leonardo or the musculature of a Michelangelo!

In 1921, speaking to teachers of the newly-founded Waldorf high school, Rudolf Steiner spoke of the relationship of beauty and sensuality:

If a child has not had the feeling for beauty awakened in him, has not been educated to see the world from an aesthetic point of view, then that boy or girl will at this age of life [adolescence] tend to become sensual, even erotic. There is no better way of restraining eroticism than by a healthy development of the aesthetic sense, a feeling for what is noble and beautiful in nature.

It is no accident that artistic activity is synonymous with creative activity. The creative powers of the human being are capable of being channeled in many directions; it is due only to the coarseness of our age that the sexual expression of these powers is so stressed. A youngster who creates on the artistic level, whose powers of body and soul are focussed on giving birth to a work of art, will go very far in sublimating those nascent procreative powers. As in any genuine loving relationship, those creative forces expended on an artistic opus reflect back upon the creator and yield objective self-knowledge.

Remember the "Sexual Revolution?" Since that time we have tended to believe that only we in our modern age know how to deal with sex. We are led to think that all ages before ours were plagued with inhibitions and chauvinism, while the last decades of the twentieth century were a period of liberation. If this is so, then why are we so plagued by sexual dysfunction and sexual diseases? Do we really want to educate our children in such a way that they join into this (at the very least) problematic approach to some of life's most basic questions?

The Renaissance runs parallel with the "Age of Discovery," a time of bold exploration of the outer world which corresponds to the inner explorations of the great artists. During this same historical period, the "Age of Natural Science" had begun as well. It was at this time that such great scientists as Francis Bacon and Galileo withdrew scientific investigation from the moral realm and exalted quantitative measurements over qualitative judgments. It was at this time, too, that anatomical researchers like Leonardo da Vinci and Fallopio thoroughly investigated the physical phenomenon of human sexual reproduction. And it was at this time that venereal disease first appeared in the civilized world. The cold and clinical scientific study of sex and the problem of sexually-transmitted diseases seem to walk hand in hand through history.

I am not saying that sex should never be mentioned in the classroom: the question is not so much whether it should be discussed, but rather how and when. As to the "how": The class teacher becomes a trusted adult to the Waldorf student, and it is natural that these students would address many important questions to such a "role model." In the course of individual conversations the class teacher can be of great help in addressing any uncertainties or confusion that youngsters might have. He is able to help because, knowing the children as well as he does he can often see beyond the "apparent" question to the real question that underlies it. So many sexual concerns and problems are really questions of destiny, variants on the questions of, "Who am I? Where do I come from? Is it possible to fully unite with another human being?" The class teacher will so couch his answers that moral warmth, rather than cold "objectivity," will be awakened in the youngster's soul.

And as to the "when": In those few Waldorf schools that go beyond eighth grade, a number of innovative courses have been created to deal with questions of love, marriage, family and, under this threefold umbrella, questions of sex as well. Steiner gave virtually no indications for the teaching of this subject, so the work that goes on in this field is still in the exciting experimental stage, and its long-term results have not been assessed; whether there is any way to assess them is a question in itself! In several of those schools lacking a high school, class teachers have attempted to approach the subject in seventh or eighth grade—usually at the request of the class parents. (It is interesting that nowadays we begin with the assumption that parents will not—or even can not—teach their own children about sexuality!) Here again, it is difficult to say in general whether such efforts have proven to be of value.

In all cases, however, before seventh grade our great concern is protecting children from society's obsession with sex. By creating a healthy social atmosphere, permeated by the love borne by the teacher for every child in the class, we are able to preserve our students' innocence to a remarkable degree in our culture.

Here, of course, we need the help of parents, supporting our efforts by carefully restricting their children's exposure to the media. The effect of the powerful combination of sight and sound on the impressionable nature of the child—via films, videos, rock music and advertising—can lead to a premature awakening of the forces of adolescence. A concern about "accelerated maturation" is probably one of the important factors that led many families to Waldorf education in the first place. Giving the child the space and time to be a child is the highest priority for a Waldorf school.

If we think for a moment about growth and development in the animal world, we see that animals have a very short "infancy," a "childhood" of only several months' duration and move rapidly towards sexual maturation—their equivalent of "adolescence." Once the animal is able to reproduce its own kind, its growth and development cease, for it never incorporates any principle higher than the astral body. The animal that has not been trained in the first year of its life will be far less able to "learn new tricks" thereafter, for with its adolescence comes the advent of old age.

In the human realm, we have a long infancy, an early, middle and late childhood, followed in turn by adolescence, which marks only the beginning of our life as an individual. Our true development as independent human beings begins at the very point where animal development ends. When this slow growth is accelerated, when the lengthy and discrete stages of childhood are compressed or even skipped, we are on the way to becoming animalic.

Once again, I realize that I am turning some of the best-intentioned "advances" in education on their heads. Rather than criticize all proponents of "early learning," I want only to stress that awakening an interest in sex before seventh grade would tend to contribute to the process of acceleration already faced by every child in America. If we want our children to become little adults, then we'll have to reckon with their becoming prone to adult ailments as well, including sexually-transmitted diseases. And just as importantly, we'll have to reckon with the animal nature of the human being growing stronger as the educative process is speeded up. The "dog eat dog" mentality that rules Wall Street and increasingly bares its teeth in the rest of the business world is an attitude fostered by men who were educated in the very "best" modern schools.

It is hardly possible to enter a Waldorf kindergarten and not fall in love with it! And, for the most part, the happiness and vitality of the children in the first three or four grades is sufficient to convince their parents that the Waldorf lower school offers the very best schooling. Only as puberty approaches, with its attendant problems and challenges, do parents get cold feet and wonder if the Waldorf school can really meet their child's academic and social needs.

From all that has preceded, it should be clear that the Waldorf approach is no less important to the adolescent than to the younger child. The Waldorf approach to the sciences, with its stress on phenomena and sense-experience is of the greatest help in drawing the teenager's attention out into the world. In mathematics and geometry, the union of scientific lawfulness and aesthetic beauty counterbalance the adolescent's tendency towards self-centered arbitrariness. Thus science heals solipsism, the malaise of our time.

The enthusiastic relating of biographies, so central to the Waldorf approach to history, provides the teenager with a sense of continuity and meaning. Many a youngster at this age feels alone and adrift, but the realization that others have struggled with dilemmas on the world-historical level can become a guide in facing problems on the personal level.

Cicero's dictum, "Not to know the events that preceded our birth is to remain forever a child" need not apply to teenagers in the Waldorf school. By penetrating the past in a living way, they take steps towards becoming truly adult.

The arts—painting, drawing, woodwork, handwork, music, eurythmy and drama—all provide that delicate balance between self-expression and objectivity that adolescents so sorely need. The delicate balance between subject and object, self and world, inner needs and outer demands is the keynote of genuine artistic activity. What is unique about Waldorf schools is not that they provide courses in art and courses in academics, for many fine independent schools do the same. What is unique in the Waldorf approach is that virtually all courses are at once academic and artistic, so that the adolescent is always addressed as a whole person.

I hope that what I have shared with you today renews your confidence in the Waldorf method, not only for the younger child, but above all for the adolescent. Never have youngsters, already fragile and unsettled at this age, been so assailed and threatened by outer forces as in our time. The artistry, the humanness and above all the sanity of the Waldorf approach help it to stand as a shelter in the midst of the storms of adolescence and as a source of renewal in the turmoil of our times.

WEAVING THE SOCIAL FABRIC OF THE CLASS

A Lecture Given at the Waldorf Institute, Spring Valley, New York, January 27, 1989

I would like to begin by making a confession. Although I am willing to talk about this topic, I would have been far more comfortable if our theme had been something like, "Metamorphosis as Pedagogical Method in the Teaching of History, Grades Five Through Twelve," or, "Algorithms, Logarithms and the Development of Mathematical Consciousness in Adolescence." Such subjects would have been far easier than the one I am asked to address tonight!

I feel reasonably able to represent the Waldorf method of teaching history, or mathematics, or any one of a dozen other subjects. When it comes to the "Waldorf approach to discipline," however, I know all too well how often I fall short, both as representative and above all as practitioner.

I say this in part because I am not only a Waldorf teacher, but, like many of you present tonight, I am the parent of Waldorf students as well. And, as a liberal, egalitarian all-American parent, I often fail miserably at disciplining my own children. As a parent, I am with my children early in the morning and late in the evening, when they and I are least awake or most fatigued. I am with them when they are hungry, or thirsty, or assailed by the thousands of temptations that constitute modern culture. When they catch me at the wrong moment, I say things I wish I hadn't said. I sometimes make threats that I can't possibly carry out, and occasionally make promises that I can't possibly keep. Far too often, I forget the ideals I hold most dear and the principles I know to be most beneficial and act merely out of expediency.

If I were speaking only as a parent, the preceding confession would pretty much constitute this lecture. Speaking as a teacher, I have more to say—but I hope that nothing I have revealed so far in inspires anything but commiseration among you. It is certainly not my intention to inspire guilt! Every parent has a formidable task facing him or her, a task which doesn't really grow any easier with the passing of time or the accumulation of experience.

To the parent is given the task of helping the child meet his karma under all of the most stressful and demanding circumstances in life, while the teacher is generally asked to work with the child only when conditions are optimum. For example, when a child is ill and develops a fever, he does not go to school, but remains home in the parent's care. Teachers usually meet the children in the controlled and aesthetic environment of their own classroom; it is the parents who must deal with the youngsters in the trying and ugly settings of shopping malls, interstate highways and fast-food restaurants.

So let this preamble be understood as a tribute to parents, the child's first educators and the unsung advocates of harmony and order in an increasingly uncivilized world. I will now be speaking primarily as a Waldorf teacher. Much of what I will say is first and foremost addressed to teachers, and neither can nor should pass over into a home situation. However, I hope that some of what is described tonight can give parents the insight or inspiration which they can creatively apply in their own way.

The title of this lecture, "Weaving the Social Fabric of the Class," brings to mind a remark that the British writer Carlyle once made about the difference between youth and old age. He said that when we are young, our life unfolds like a beautiful tapestry. When we grow old, we are permitted to step behind the tapestry. It is no longer so beautiful, but at last we can see all of the threads, and follow their connections!

Many of those present tonight have beheld the tapestry of the life of a Waldorf school as it manifests itself in class plays, in assemblies, in concerts and in the social experiences generated by parent evenings and class outings. Tonight, like Carlyle's old man, we will step behind the impressive tapestry to view the threads. By no means are they all neatly tied together, but at least we will glean something of the grand design that underlies our work, and view some of the strands that remain to be woven into this "work in progress."

One thread that will wind its way through tonight's lecture is the statement made by Rudolf Steiner that, just as imitation of the world around "educates" the child before the change of teeth, so between grades one and eight, authority is the primary educative power. What did he mean by this?

Rather than answer directly, I would like to share with you the following dramatic re-enactment. It is a composite of scenes that I have witnessed again and again in Waldorf classrooms throughout America (We are in a second grade classroom at "circle time," when the children sing, recite poetry or play rhythmic games. The teacher stands before his class, about to lead them in a new poem):

> All right, could everyone please stand up? We'll try to recite our verse about the dragon. Please—could we all get out of our seats and stand? Could we also quiet down a little?
>
> All right, we're almost all quiet, so I guess we'll go ahead. . . Now, could we all try to clap our hands? Prescott, why aren't you standing? Why aren't you doing as I asked? What do you mean, you don't want to stand up? Please, Prescott, try to do as I've asked. . .
>
> Second graders, could you all be quiet while I talk to Prescott? Now, let's begin, shall we? Sativa, why are you sitting down? You're terribly fatigued? But, it's the beginning of the day! Couldn't you just try standing up along with the others? You think that you have Chronic Fatigue Syndrome? Now, Sativa, I never heard of anyone your age suffering from such an. . . Clay, how do you know that I'm wrong? Second graders, please

be quiet while Clay and Sativa and I are talking! Now, listen, Clay, just because you saw that on PBS doesn't make it absolutely true! Has anyone else here ever heard of a second grader with CFS?—

Ezekiel, will you please leave the room? Yes, I mean it! I won't have you pulling Natasha's hair while I— Second graders, please be quiet! All right, all right, could everybody please sit down; we'll say the verse from our desks. Yes, that's it, could you all return to your seats? Good. Now for our verse— Prescott, why are you still standing?

And so it goes, on and on, day after day, in classrooms from coast to coast!

What is the nature of the problem here? First of all, this "composite teacher's" misguided approach is to be a friend to his second graders, rather than an authority. I think that I can speak for my whole generation—those of us who were born in the post World War II years—when I say that, as the children of adults who rejected the authoritarian ways of their elders, we grew up experiencing little of parental authority, and therefore are ill-equipped to act as authorities to anyone else.

Notice that I am distinguishing between being authoritarian and acting out of authority; very often, in America, the two are confused, and so we have that phrase held over from the 'Sixties: "Question Authority!" Whether or not we, as individualized adults, enjoy questioning or challenging authority, it is incumbent upon us as Waldorf teachers to serve as authorities for our children. Between seven and fourteen the child craves authority for the sake of his soul development and needs authority so that he may have an outer form in which to incarnate.

Our harried second grade teacher throws another obstacle in his own path when he makes threats but does not act upon them. How much better not to make the threat at all, but to simply perform the action! Think of how much aggravation teachers would be spared in the course of a day if they made their motto, "Deeds, not words!" If we take seriously the thought that young children live most intensely in their feeling and will organizations, the "language of gesture" can eloquently communicate our intentions and concerns.

A threat is pedagogically problematic because it implies a cause-and-effect relationship which will transpire over the course of time. Yet as Waldorf teachers we should recognize that the child's relationship to the course of time is still quite dreamlike, and his comprehension of causal relationships is virtually nonexistent. Voicing threats to children in third grade or below is a denial of those same childlike qualities that Waldorf teachers are meant to be cultivating.

Even with older children, threats have a way of piling up, like MX missiles in their silos, and once we've unleashed our weapons, well, what remains in the arsenal? Either you continue to escalate, finally threatening to use the Ultimate Weapon of suspension, or expulsion or something similar—or you go back on your threat, recognizing that matters have gotten out of hand. In so doing, you weaken your credibility, and once the children's confidence in your word is gone, you have lost most of the battle for their hearts.

It might be good to recall here the anecdote about Annie Sullivan, Helen Keller's teacher. To an admirer who told her, "You worked miracles with Helen because you got her to love you," Annie Sullivan replied, "No; first Helen had to learn to obey me. Obedience came first, then came love."

And last, but not least, in this litany of errors is this teacher's habitual use of the interrogative sentence instead of the declarative statement. "All right, could everyone please stand up? Please—could we all get out of our seats and stand? Could we also quiet down a little? Now, let's begin, shall we?" How much clearer and more to the point it would be to say, "Please stand up, class," or "Please quiet down," or "We are about to begin!" When a question is asked of a child, he assumes that you expect an answer, and I have heard many children answer questions like the above with witty or even downright rude answers!

If you want the class to stand up, then tell it (politely) to stand up. If you want the class to be seated, then tell it so. If you are not sure whether you want the class to stand or to sit, then what in the world are doing up there in front of them? Dear teachers—and, I might add, dear parents, for this is one lesson learned in the classroom that you can take home with you—Children do not need choices; they need guidance.

We know that so much that is basic in Waldorf education rests on the understanding that whatever in our childhood acts upon us from without will in adulthood be transformed into forces that work from within. A child who lacks the living example of a self-assured and guiding adult will have to struggle, in later life, to attain inner assurance and inner guidance. A youngster who is not exposed to the kind but clear precepts of outer discipline will find it difficult to attain true inner discipline as an adult. If we cannot steel ourselves so that we meet the children with certainty in our will and clarity in our intentions, we are depriving them of one of childhood's most valuable experiences.

In the United States, which, after all, is a nation founded on the Divine right of freedom of choice, it is a mighty task indeed to overcome this dogged tendency to ask children questions! Our whole culture summons forth the interrogative voice:

> "Time to wake up! Do you want to wear your Jordache shorts or your Guess jeans? Would you like the Chanel sweater or the Polo shirt? Ready for breakfast? What will it be: Cheerios, Corn Flakes, Wheaties, Granola...How about strawberries? No? Blueberries? Bananas? Do you want to sweeten it with honey? You want sugar? White or brown?..."

I needn't go on, because the look of consternation that I see on many of your faces tells me that I have, unfortunately, hit home.

May I repeat that I am not trying to give you pangs of guilt, for this monologue could just as easily have come from my home as from yours! Such domestic scenes are part of the dilemma of raising children in a country that rightfully calls itself "The Land of the Free," but has lost the capacity to distinguish between the independent, "free" adult and the highly dependent and "unfree" child. You may ask then, "But isn't Waldorf Education an 'education towards freedom'?" The operational word here is *towards*. True freedom is a capacity which can unfold only in adults, and even then only in rare moments, for life is filled with necessities that impinge upon our freedom.

When we ask a child to make a choice, several things occur. First of all, we ask the child to draw upon capacities for judgment that he does not yet have. On what basis will a seven year-old make a choice? Invariably, on the basis of sympathy and antipathy. And whence does he get this sympathy and antipathy? From his astral body, that is, from a member of his being that should not be activated until adolescence. The youngster who is always choosing one thing and rejecting another is drawing on "soul capital" that should be kept in the spiritual bank to gather interest for several more years. When such a child needs those astral forces in their fullness at age fourteen or fifteen, they may be depleted.

In that moment of choice, the adult who gives the choice relinquishes the majesty and power that should be hers by dint of experience and acquired wisdom. For that moment, child and adult are equal;

over the course of many such moments of choice, this equality becomes habitual, and the sweetest children gradually turn into little tyrants who wield the power to determine the restaurants in which the family will eat, the movies that they will see, the malls in which they will shop. We don't have to watch situation comedies on TV to experience the ubiquity of such children in modern life!

Most importantly, we should realize that a child who is given too many choices will become an adult who has difficulty making decisions. While choice, according to definition, "implies broadly the freedom of choosing from a set of persons or things," decision is defined as "the act of reaching a conclusion or making up one's mind," and also, interestingly, as "firmness of character or action; determination." I don't mean to overwhelm you with scholarship, but I do want to point out the difference between these two acts. The power to decide, I would claim, is built upon the ability to accept the decisions of adults in one's youth. (This assumes, of course, that one encounters adults who are themselves capable of making decisions.) Childish choosing draws on those very forces of soul and spirit that are meant to mature and become adult decisiveness.

If you are uncomfortable with such a characterization, I would suggest that you look at the current state of our generation, the postwar "baby boomers" who were allowed to become "a generation of choosers." How many contemporaries do you know who are truly decisive people? Well, don't all raise your hands at once! Now, how many of your friends have difficulty deciding even the smallest matters, not to speak of making such major life decisions as, whom should I marry (or unmarry)? what should my vocation be? what am I going to do with the rest of my life?

Your smiles tell me that I'm describing individuals well-known to you—individuals, we must remember, who very likely had doting, progressive parents who wanted them to be happy and gave them as many choices as possible! The effect of such indecisiveness can be amusing, but it has its serious consequences as well. With disturbing frequency, one guru or Master after another passes through our country and charismatically draws a host of followers to his community or ashram. Some of those drawn are simple, easily-influenced souls who can barely manage their own lives. However, a surprising number of these disciples are intelligent, highly-educated "professionals," who willingly relinquish their right to make any decisions about the rest of their lives, believing that their teacher is far better able to do so.

Isn't that interesting? Members of the *creme de la creme* of the Generation of Choosers, having arrived at mature adulthood, now search for the decisive teacher that they lacked in their childhood!

The simplicity of life in earlier days was accompanied by a lack of choices—which we would today find boring—but this in turn led to a consistency of life which we might find healing. This is no turning back from the "freedom of choice" that we as adults expect, but we must recognize that a pre-determined and expectable course of events strengthens the etheric body of the child, and it is this which provides a sturdy foundation for the making of important decisions in later life.

We can encompass the child with our own certainty by creating a form into which the child enters every day. Even on the first day of first grade, it makes a great difference whether the children haphazardly deposit jackets and lunchbags all over the classroom, or find that their teacher has labeled coat hooks and cubbies with their initials or their particular symbol. The assigning of desks ahead of time, the labeling of crayon boxes and recorder cases: all of this tells the children (without words) that a space has been made for them, a form has been created, and they are warmly welcomed to fill it. Asking the children themselves to choose coat hooks, cubbies, desks etc. will lead to conflict and irresolution—before you have even begun to teach a thing!

The fostering of healthy rhythms is another means by which we protect the child from having to choose. The Waldorf classroom is permeated by rhythmical activities. The lighting of the candle and recitation of the daily verse, the singing of songs at a prescribed time each day, followed by the telling of story, followed by drawing and so on; as the weeks go by, the child's etheric body forms itself in the image of these rhythms, and we find that we have created rituals.

In the midst of life's uncertainties and

indecisiveness, from which not even children are spared today, such rituals give clear contours to an otherwise amorphous existence. In such a rhythmic setting a child does not have to ask, "What are we doing today?" or, worse yet, be asked by an adult, "What do you want to do today?" If it is the beginning of Main Lesson, we light the candle. If it is Tuesday, we model with beeswax. If it is lunchtime, we eat lunch, and neither sooner nor later.

For this to unfold harmoniously, of course, the teacher will have to think out many things in advance and carefully plan the school year, the week, the day. He must decide what his intentions are, decide how he will carry them out, and plan out in advance how to best help individual children find their way to the form. The teacher must choose, to spare the children the burden of choice.

When in this way the teacher serves as the "Guardian of Form" in the life of the classroom, he creates the preconditions for the healthy social life of the class. "Discipline" comes from the word "discipleship," and the disciple is by definition one who follows religiously and devotedly the decisions made by his master. It will follow, as does the day the night, that a classroom permeated by a healthy sense of order, a vital feeling for form, will be a space in which more disciplined behavior will be seen.

To prevent any misunderstanding, I must stress that I am here speaking about the first three grades. Once the child has gone through the "nine year-old change" we should begin to present him with some choices—not too many, mind you!—but enough to stimulate the slumbering inner life that should now begin to awaken. As with all aspects of Waldorf education, our stress on one quality or another, one method or another, holds for a certain age range and then must be developed or transformed.

Human history points to this as well. In the earliest stage of the history of every major culture we find theocracy, the rulership of the priests. Acting as the representatives of the gods, the priests make all decisions and dictate virtually every detail of life. In this respect, the Waldorf kindergarten is theocratic in nature, and the very important people who teach there are the High Priests of the school—although they may have to relinquish this privilege at faculty meetings!

A second stage is that of the monarchy, the rule of kings. In the Old Testament, the transition from Samuel to Saul gives us a clear picture of the tremendous importance that the transition from theocracy to monarchy held for the Hebrew people. The king rules no longer as God's deputy, but rather as one who embodies all that is highest in mankind itself. To his people he is at once ruler and servant, judge and general. He is decisive, yet he must also be just. Here we find the "archetype" of the Class Teacher. I might add that anyone who has attended a Lower School meeting in which something controversial was being discussed would have no question that he was hearing eight kings (and queens), each quite accustomed to ruling his own domain!

The third historical stage should take us to the

peaceful transition from monarchy to democracy—but how rare are the instances in which this transition is made peacefully! In most cases, this step is made through protest and revolution, and we will be safe to assume that the same would hold true in a Waldorf school. This stage occurs somewhere between seventh grade and ninth grade, as the child becomes an adolescent and the revolution he experiences in his own body and soul cries out for external expression. Now (he believes) he need no longer follow decisions made from "on high," but must be left free to choose for himself. The wise teacher will begin presenting options and creating situations in which choice is possible. Never, however, should the teacher abdicate his final responsibility for making—and standing behind—the most essential decisions in the classroom, for young teenagers still crave guidance. Relinquish your role as an adult and, as in the French Revolution, a Reign of Teenage Terror will follow!

* * * * * *

Up until now, we have been looking at the teacher's relationship to his class very much in terms of the life of willing. I would like us to now look at this same relationship from the vantage point of the life of feeling. In regard to her life of feeling, the grade school child is very much affected by an environment filled with beauty, which in turn stimulates feelings of gratitude and love.

This may all sound rather vague and sentimental,

but in Rudolf Steiner's ideas concerning child psychology even the most ineffable feelings can be approached with clarity. The notion of beauty that we generally have today has to do with matters of personal taste, fashion and relativism: it is the diametric opposite of functionalism. Yet to Steiner beauty was so functional that he once stated that, if our cities were architecturally beautiful places in which to live, crime would disappear! This is, indeed, an astonishing proposition, but in America we are testing its converse and are finding it, tragically, to be true.

So to develop healthy social feelings among the children, we try to create a beautiful environment in our classrooms and in our schools. We should remember, of course, that beauty doesn't lie only in hand-dyed silken cloths, gleaming crystals and sculptured wooden frames around our blackboards, aesthetically pleasing though these may be. It resides also in the order that lives in the classroom space, in its neatness and in its cleanliness.

It is interesting to observe what a difficult time we Waldorf teachers have keeping our house in order! Though we may be painfully aware of the effect of inharmonious colors and synthetic fabrics on our children and our selves, we can be oblivious to the equally powerful effect of an undusted desk, an unwatered plant, or school supplies thrown haphazardly into a closet (Although the door is shut, the mess is there anyway!). Rudolf Steiner has gone into great detail concerning the various types of elemental beings who inhabit different kinds of environments, and has mentioned the particularly aggressive elementals who "fight in the dust." Might this mean that a dusty and disorderly classroom, by virtue of its elementality, could actually encourage unrest and even fighting? We see how "beauty" is not so vague a notion after all, but is in its way as indispensable as a properly functioning thermostat.

I have always felt that Class Teachers have a lot to learn about beauty and order from our colleagues in the Kindergarten. The "nourishment of the senses," which is actually the nutritional stream that builds up the substance of the child's body, is an art and a science among the Kindergarten teachers, and I am obliged to them for many helpful hints about my classroom environment. And, of course, we should not leave ourselves out of the child's environment. For a good part of every main lesson, our children are focussing on us, and we should make every effort to "dress up" for school, with an eye to color, form and (at least in the upper grades) even fashion!

A beautiful drawing on the blackboard, appropriate works of art on the walls, crystals, shells, a finely-wrought candle snuffer next to a handmade candle-holder and other treasures on the teacher's desk; a cared-for "nature table" reflecting the seasons, chalk and crayons in order, class materials in wicker baskets, or wooden trays, or cloth bags: each of us has his own picture of that aesthetically complete classroom in which the Ideal of Beauty can fully incarnate. Cultivate that ideal and strive to realize it! Not only will it be a feast for your children's senses, but it will become yet another cornerstone for the social foundation of the class.

Through cultivating beauty in the children's surroundings, we begin to awaken gratitude in their souls, but, as with all other soul qualities, "only that which is nourished will grow." To nourish and encourage gratitude among our students, we must show that we also possess it. It is more than coincidence that the words "gratitude" and "greeting" are similar, although they are not etymologically connected. For the way in which we greet the children in the morning (as well as the way in which we dismiss them at the day's end) can be an expression of the gratitude we feel for their presence in our class.

We must acknowledge the sorry fact that too many children have little in the way of conversation with their parents or sibling first thing in the morning. Given the hectic pace of the average household and the pervasiveness of the media, the morning voice of a favorite disc jockey or newscaster may be more familiar—or comforting—than the morning voice of a very busy parent. The teacher's morning greeting must then be all the more filled with warmth and thankfulness. As you shake a child's hand, let the tone of your voice, your smile or a personal remark tell her that you are glad that she has chosen to awaken once again, that you are glad that she is alive, or, if she is choleric, that she is bursting with life—we must be filled, every day, with gratitude for the incarnation process itself!

That we can bring such gratitude daily to our classroom is possible only because we attempt to perceive that proverbial "hook" that Rudolf Steiner told us stood outside of our room. Upon that hook we hang, like a heavy old coat, all that is merely personal and self-involved in our being, so that we can stand before our children filled with thanks; thanks for the world, for our task in the world, and for the children who make it all so necessary.

If we can radiate our feeling of gratitude towards the children, it will reflected back manyfold. In the first three grades, of course, every child lives in something of a dream; he is hardly aware of the physical or soul differences between himself and the others, and social life is governed completely from the outside by parents and teachers. Like so many seeds, the feelings of adults are planted within the dreamer's soul to sprout and grow in the middle grades and flower in the High School years. If you convey an evenhanded, objective and grateful attitude towards every child in the class, you will have gone far in opening the way for social understanding among the youngsters when they reach adolescence.

There is little in a classroom that causes more harm than the involuntary change in the tone of the teacher's voice when he is addressing a "difficult" student. A voice with an edge to it, a tone of sarcasm, a tinge of irritation—which of us hasn't spoken too often out of a spirit of pettiness and negativity? If we accept Steiner's notion that the teacher's voice is one of the greatest formative powers in the life of the child, I needn't say much more about the importance of controlling not only our tongues but also our tones when we speak to our children. Our students will never speak to one another with any more kindness than they have learned from us, whereas even a hint of malice on our part has the nefarious quality of being amplified beyond all measure.

Another way of helping the children to awaken to the very best in one another is to encourage children to listen to each other. Here we see how wise it is to absolutely insist that no one speak without raising his hand and waiting his turn (This is a rule in every classroom I've ever visited, but, as Hamlet said, it is honored mostly in the breach.). When one child speaks, then insist that everyone else listen. As the children grow older, have them come up to the front of the room and speak to the entire class, and demand that everyone give the individual child the kind of full attention that they would give to you. It's all so terribly prosaic, and it's not as though these are even "Waldorf" ideas! I would contend, however, that a teacher who adheres to these simple rules and procedures will go a long way in facing the terrible "communication problems" that underlie so many social conflicts in our time. In learning to listen to one another, our youngsters learn to respect one another and to develop tolerance for the most diverse points of view.

Developing such habits in the classroom will require patience, and it will above all take time. The "review" part of a third grade main lesson may take much longer if we ask a shy child to come up to the front and if we must wait for her classmates to grow quiet and so forth. We may have to work with greater discipline and economy to teach all of the content that we have prepared. Yet what content could be of greater import for the future of our students—and, by inference, the future of the world—than developing a "social sense"?

Another part of the classroom's "social fabric" that is often threadbare—if not downright ragged—has to do with the children's eating habits. Most of us preside over two mealtimes in the course of the day: snacktime, which follows main lesson, and lunchtime. First, the children open their lunchboxes or wicker baskets and see and smell their food, which stimulates the nerve/sense organization. Each meal is preceded by a grace (another word which echoes "gratitude" and "greeting") which is spoken or sung—so it is connected with our breath or rhythmic organization. The grace is followed by eating, which is itself followed by digesting, which is connected with the metabolic/limb organization. I point to these obvious facts only because it is the obvious which is sometimes so mysterious in the life of the child.

So every meal contains an interesting progression. First the child awakens in his head, and we hope that he perceives food that is beautiful to look upon, and that exudes a pleasing aroma. Next, out of the reverence of his soul, the child expresses thanks. Last, a part of his being in which he is completely asleep goes to work so that the food can be assimilated. From the head, to the heart, to the lower organs. From thinking, to feeling, to willing.

If we exclude the phlegmatics, for whom snack and lunch are almost rapturous experiences, we will find that many children eat a little and then begin to talk. No sooner does the talk begin, but that it grows mirthful, then silly, and then, much to our surprise, a certain meanness creeps in. Before too long we may find that many of the children are engaged in loud, uproarious shouting, while one or two are in tears, the victims of unpleasant remarks made by classmates. The social fabric of the class, woven so laboriously over the two hour-long main lesson, is rapidly rent asunder.

How does this happen? I would suggest that the difficulties arise as the chewed foodstuff leaves the more "wakeful" zone of the mouth and rhythmic system and enters the zone of "sleep," the digestive organs proper. Rudolf Steiner tells us in his cycle The Influence of Spiritual Beings Upon Man (1908) that, as food is transformed into chyle, elemental beings connected to Venus are active. Depending on the type of food and the quality of food that a child eats, the active beings will either be of the amiable, gentle Venus type, or the "evil" Venus beings, "who present a wild and furious vitality, and whose principal occupation consists in mutual fighting and plunder."

A frightening picture, yet one that describes all too vividly the unbridled behavior that we witness at a classroom mealtime! It is not the children who are fighting; it is the elemental world in conflict, the forces of food in battle. In recent weeks a new kind of "action figure toy" has been released to join the host of plastic demons inhabiting children's nurseries and bedrooms. Called the "Food Fighters," they are cleverly molded replicas of hamburgers, french fries etc. with horrific, malevolent faces and limbs designed to strike an aggressive stance.

Given the degree of industrial processing our foodstuffs go through on the farm and in the factory, we can safely assume that our children are carrying their fair share of "Food Fighters." We abdicate our responsibility for them when we adopt a laissez-faire attitude towards snack and lunchtimes. It is essential for us to consciously draw the good, "gentle and amiable" Venus forces around the children, to counteract the influence of the malicious elementals.

What does Venus rule? In ancient times, Venus was the planet whose inhabiting goddess ruled Love. We have seen how the meal begins with gratitude, as we lead the children in a grace. We must now lead the children towards love, the second great pillar of the grade school years.

To help the children overcome the negative Venus forces, we can consider taking the following steps: Rather than let the children remain at their desks while they eat, create small social groupings that change every week or two, so that new friendships can be made. Try to created temperamentally "balanced" groups, so that phlegmatics can help the choleric eaters slow down, and melancholics can make sure that the sanguines finish their sandwiches! Eat with your children, and converse with them! The art of conversation, which in Goethe's tale of The Green Snake was accounted "more precious than gold," is becoming a lost art. Come as prepared to lead lovely mealtime conversations as you are to lead main lesson: "Last night I saw a raccoon in my back yard!" "Did anyone have frost on his window this morning?" "I'm going away this weekend!" And, last but not least, throughout the meal adhere to rules of decent etiquette (another lost art!). Remind the children that their classroom is not a fast-food hangout and that eating is a civilized activity.

This "mealtime therapy" is another one of those healings required in our time because so much in our culture runs counter to health. The fast-food restaurants mentioned above—which certainly take the "rest" out of the "restaurant"—and the pervasive habit families have of eating while watching TV, snacking individually etc.; all of this makes eating an anti-social activity. Think of the importance of the feast in old stories, where people strove to be at their best and most noble. Or, more significantly, think of the "Last Supper" that archetype of earthly social life, where Love is at once the "host" and the "guest" and the substance of the meal. Improving the tenor of the snacktimes and lunchtimes will slowly form yet another cornerstone of our social foundation.

At this point someone might object, "This talk about beauty, gratitude and love is well and good, but what about the child who is insensitive to the classroom environment, who mocks the mealtime grace and who rejects the efforts of other children to be friendly?"

We are describing here the child I would term the "class outsider." This outsider can take on various forms, some of which are related to the four temperaments. There is the Sanguine Outsider, who is often something of a "prima donna" type. She is always late, but instead of quietly entering the room she brazenly makes sure that her presence is announced and registered! She flaunts her possessions, her snack foods, her daddy's car and her mommy's jewels, seemingly oblivious to the negative response she elicits from her classmates.

The Phlegmatic Outsider, on the other hand, is quiet to the point of inertness. He is usually big, perhaps fat, and this physical substantiality by itself makes him stand out in the class. His size and attendant slowness make him the butt of jokes, which, while gentle at first, escalate alarmingly in their cruelty. Unable to respond quickly, he gradually falls into a sleep in relation to his classmates, and eventually his teacher; he grows uninvolved in life and learning.

We meet the Choleric Outsider the very first day of school; indeed, usually in the very first minute. He craves our attention, and will scream, hit, cry or wreak havoc in a hundred other ways until he has gotten it. He is unaware of the rapid movement of his limbs, so he rams into classmates, or pummels them, or pinches them in it seems) complete innocence. He disrupts every story, he mocks every prayer and, in counterpoint to the "beautiful speech" cultivated by the teacher, he recites a litany of bad, bad words.

The Melancholic Outsider challenges us with a "double whammy." By their very nature melancholics, like the color blue, prefer the edges and corners of life, observing rather than joining. The Melancholic Outsider can become the classroom pariah, exuding darkness so deep that no one wants to go near her. She shuns her classmates' company, preferring her "invisible friends," who often have a bizarre quality about them. She may be the class pack rat, eagerly collecting the crayon shavings and bottle caps that the other children throw away and hoarding them like a dragon's treasure.

If these four types—whom, I believe, you can all recognize—have any one quality in common, it is this: they all appear to be completely uninvolved in the life of the class. In a regular classroom, this would not necessarily become an impediment, but in a Waldorf school classroom, involvement is everything. And just as I noted a common strand uniting the words "gratitude" and "greeting," I would like to connect the words involved and loved.

These children are outsiders because they feel themselves to be unloved; whether they are unloved in reality is not important, because the child's feelings are all that is real to him. As children who do not believe that they are receiving love, they are in turn incapable of giving love to others. This "unloved child", dear parents and teachers, is the most handicapped kind of child that we will ever meet! I don't care how high an IQ she has, how wealthy his parents are, or how articulate she is—a child who does not receive and cannot give love is deeply disabled.

It is one of the telling points of our difficult age that the ranks of these "outsiders" are growing. Every one of you has—or has had—such a child, or several such children in your class. Each teacher must find his own way to relate to the sometimes heartrending difficulties the outsider presents. When thinking about the teacher's relationship to these children, I find myself paraphrasing what the Clown in Shakespeare's *Twelfth Night* says about "greatness": "Some teachers are born to take on such problems, some teachers become able to take on such problems—and some teachers have such problems thrust upon them." I suspect that most of us belong in the third category!

It is essential, I believe, that no one feel guilty if he or she is not able to work with such a child and decides that the class as a whole would be better off if the outsider left. Indeed, were we able to look deeply, we might at times discover that the karma of that outsider did not really "mesh" with the karma of his classmates. On the other hand, we would be wrong to simply assume that "Waldorf schools aren't meant to handle difficult children," and hold up the archetypical blonde, blue-eyed child who draws well, is good in music, obeys the teacher etc. as the only kind of child we are meant to accept! The children we can help, the children we can't—it is all so bound up with our destiny, and we must make such careful and considered judgments!

If, however, you do choose to work with such an outsider, which means that you have chosen to follow a path of Love, there are several things to consider. For one, you will probably be assailed by parents and other teachers who are convinced that such a difficult child is undermining the rest of the class. You will hear that, if she were to leave, there would be a rapid improvement in: a) class discipline, b) the class's achievement level, c) the children's language and d) the happiness and well-being of all the other children.

That's a pretty tall order! Would you ever have believed that one little eight or nine year-old could be responsible for so much misery? You may laugh about it now, but just wait until those parents and colleagues start calling you up or ambushing you on the parking lot, telling you that, if that troublesome child doesn't leave the class, their child will! And you'll have to admit that, yes, they're correct in many ways, they're awake to the seriousness of the problem, but, on the other hand...doesn't everyone need a scapegoat?

For, after all, what really does happen when a very difficult child leaves a class? Every situation is different, but, in general, the teacher finds he can breathe again. The children seem relieved, the parents and colleagues are grateful, all goes as smoothly as they had predicted and then. . . Wonder of wonders—another child starts to behave just like the "outsider" who left! Within a few weeks or months, you have a former "insider" transformed into an "outsider," and a new set of parents demanding his immediate expulsion. The class dynamic, it seems, has a will of its own!

Once again, let me state the obvious: the outer life of the class is a reflection of the inner life of the teacher. The entire Waldorf method is predicated on this perhaps disquieting fact. This places that "outsider" in a very different light, does it not? Perhaps it is she who, most attuned to your innermost being, has taken on those dark spaces that would not otherwise surface. The "outsider," in this respect, may be the ultimate insider, the child most intimately connected with her teacher, "warts and all."

I have no intention of giving you generalized solutions to the problem of such difficult children, because, by their very nature, every "outsider" is truly unique. And if what I imply above is correct, at least part of the solution to that problem child "out there" will lie in confronting the problem child "in here"—in your own heart and soul. Such children are like guides, sent from on high, to lead us to what older cultures called the "Secret of the Shadow," or to what Rudolf Steiner called the "Mystery of the Double."

The child giving you the most trouble is probably your best guide! Look at it this way: Shakespeare has given us a great tragedy, *Macbeth*. Within that drama stands Lady Macbeth. She is vengeful and ambitious, she is a murderess, and she eventually succumbs to what we would term paranoid delusions and commits suicide. She is not much of a role model, but what would the tragedy of Macbeth be without her? How could the action move forward with such sustained dramatic pitch were it not for this most unpleasant, difficult and evil character?

Great dramas can serve as object lessons for class teachers, for in a great drama every character has his part to play and every part is essential. We admire a Shakespeare or a Molière not because they shower us with sunny sentiments of universal sweetness, but because of their ability to delineate the full range of human character. Can we say something similar about ourselves?

Can we say that even though we can't create many shades of human disposition, at least we are able to teach a full range of personalities? We need to get in the habit of experiencing our classroom as a stage upon which many actors are playing their roles. Why each has chosen his or her particular part is, to begin with, no more our concern than it is when we watch a theatre performance; we begin by accepting that each actor is as well cast as possible. Unlike the theatre, however, we are present not merely as a member of the audience, but also as stage manager, director, coach and prompter. On occasion we may even be asked to play a minor role.

If now and then we view our classroom in this way, the role of the outsider, of the exceptionally difficult child becomes that much more comprehensible. The impact of this grand drama—this "slice of life"—would be weakened through the absence of any of the players, but somehow it is the ornery characters who provide the greatest momentum. And as I mentioned above, your role is anything but passive! It is up to you to provide the greatest number of interactions between the players, to help each actor take a thorough hold of his role, and also to help each actor live into everyone else's role with understanding and sympathy. The greatest actors know that their parts exist in between them and their fellow actors, in between them and their audience. It is this interplay, this dynamic that makes the classroom come to life.

Emerson said, in his Spiritual Laws, "Every man has this call of the power to do somewhat unique, and no man has any other call." Please consider this when the moment of truth arrives and you must consider whether or not a child "belongs" in your class. Certainly, there are times when a child cannot be carried any more by a teacher—but this is true far less frequently than we would think!

Indeed, if we can be certain of anything in this mad and unpredictable world, it is that difficult and needy children will be coming our way in ever greater numbers. We will turn some away, but the numbers will be such that we will be compelled to accept many. Like understanding teachers, these difficult children will help to liberate us from our narrow notions of what is "normal" and "acceptable." They will open us up to the experience of the Threshold.

As I said at the beginning of this lecture, we Waldorf teachers tend to see children at their best, under the optimum conditions.

Unlike public school teachers, we also have the freedom to accept or reject children according to our lofty standards. To put it another way, we are spoiled! No wonder the thought of having a few really tough cases makes us tremble! If the idea of working with ever more difficult children causes you some trepidation, let me make a final suggestion.

Avail yourself of any opportunity to visit and/or work with two groups of people who live very close to the Threshold of the spiritual world: the severely handicapped, e.g. the retarded and emotionally disturbed and also the aged and the dying. My own life experience has included long connections with individuals from both of these groups, and I could never express fully how grateful I am for this. To work with the handicapped and the aged is to put one's own classroom experiences in a context, to relate them to the fullness and complexity of "real life."

Such work will also help us to recognize that the "worst" child in a Waldorf classroom would hardly stand out in many a public school resource room, and that the strain and stress we feel in working with a particular child's needs would pale when compared to the superhuman effort it takes to truly care for a dying person. We will all need some "context" and a lot of perspective if we wish to be ready to face the classrooms of the nineteen-nineties.

Let us strive to broaden our scope as "playwrights," to bring ever greater diversity and range into our classroom. Or let us see ourselves as weavers, working on the warp of Gratitude and the woof of Love, weaving cloths of multitextured and varicolored Beauty. There is no event so unforeseen, no child so intractable, no destiny so unredeemable that it cannot in some way be woven into this remarkable fabric, this social life of the Waldorf classroom.